Mayhem, Murder & Magnificence

A Memoir
By Ivan Kilgore

Contents

Introduction

I t is often said that everyone has a book in them; that the events of our lives become words on a page inspiring a story others will vicariously seek to experience. Often, our best-sellers reflect the stories of those who, at some point in life, discovered the ability to create and control their own narrative. Opposed to being manipulated by circumstances, they are the ones who learn how to manipulate them to their advantage. For them life is a blank page. The words they write on it are the blueprint to success, happiness, wealth, and so much more. These are the words that inspire us to wake up everyday and greet an imperfect world with sure determination to overcome the challenges it places before us.

Mayhem, Murder & Magnificence, a memoir, is an inspirational story of author, philanthropist and activist Ivan Kilgore who found inspiration to establish the United Black Family Scholarship Foundation under circumstances least likely to inspire most. Wrongfully convicted of first-degree murder and sentenced to life without the possibility of parole, he inspires readers with a unique story that tells of countless obstacles and lessons learned while navigating some of the nation's most dangerous ghettos and prisons.

A small town country boy, who dared to reach for the American dream, this is a story of triumphant and pain staking lessons learned in some of the most unthinkable predicaments a human being could find him or herself in.

Humble Beginnings

May 25th, 2020, George Floyd is murdered as the world watches the air literally being suffocated from his lungs. Four officers eventually were charged in his homicide. The outcome? Who can predict. But if contemporary history is any indicator, the likelihood of a conviction for murder is slim. Even more, any resulting conviction will be a slap on the wrist. This is the world I live in today. It is a world that still grapples with good old American racism some 46 years after I was born in 1974.

That I write this from a medium security prison cell in Northern California should come as no surprise to America. After all the social death of the African American has always been part of the American experience. It is a truism I think about too often: How did I find myself, by the age of 26, twice charged with capital murder and eventually sentenced to life without the possibility of parole? What brought me to the point of killing another black man? What circumstances created this wanton disregard of life?

It would take me years to eventually find the answers to these questions. In fact, I am still searching for answers. I guess, in part, it is why I am writing the next chapter in my life having been asked, "How is it you keep going under such circumstances?" Then they say, "You are in prison doing more than most in the streets!" I would be lying if I said prison did not inspire me, to some extent, to step up my game and learn how to see beyond the these physical (and mental) walls. But I want to be clear, prison does not always inspire people in such a way. In fact, in most cases it does not inspire at all. Nor is prison the driving force behind any measure of success I am perceived to have. My drive and success come from the values and work ethic that was instilled in me long before I set foot in a prison. I often tell people that prior to my incarceration, I was already building the foundation to be successful.

November 1998, I paroled from Cushing. Two months after my release, I was enrolled in a small Junior college in Pittsburg, California as a business major. From that point up until I was arrested and charged with first-degree murder in November of 2000, I was a full time college student. By then I had managed to get underway a small clothing store, *Ive's One Stop Shop Hip Hop Spot* in Oakland, California. Life was good. I was working with some of the biggest acts in the music business in the Bay Area.

Of course, everything was not on the level with me. I also fed the block with plenty of "trees" in West Oakland and a few other spots between and throughout the Bay Area, Atlanta, Dallas, Oklahoma City, and Los Angeles. Though, things were not as big as they seem. I was a small time hustler, just a few pounds here and there, but with big dreams as an "entra-poor-negro".

Of all places I decided to move to when I got out of prison, why Oakland, California? My Aunt Beverley. She told me it was the one place where I would truly begin to understand the impact of Southern racism.

Growing up as a kid in quiet, small town America, you really do not understand how the forces of racism and poverty interconnect to shape your reality. Sure, you see and experience them. You feel the brunt of them as well as the pain and shame they cause. Still and yet, you really do not understand just how deeply they influence your condition. Or your mindset for that much.

It was not until I was well into my thirties and setting in prison with a life sentence that I begin to understand the impact of racism, how it affected my life, my decisions, my family, history, and more importantly, my future. For me this was a process of hindsight coupled with intense study while in the Alameda County Jail, which forced me to take a deep and hard look at my humble beginnings.

I was born and raised in Wewoka, Oklahoma. Founded in 1849, I was surprised to learn it was established by the Black Seminole Indians. History tells that they were formerly runaway slaves who had escaped the plantations of Georgia and the Carolinas to ban with the Natives of the Florida Everglades. There, West African and North American Native culture would mesh into the melting pot of language, warfare and amalgamation of bloodlines. The word "Seminole" which sprung forth from the Gullah and Native tongues, literally meant "runaway". As allies, our ancestors would fight side-by-side to stave off imperialism and African slavers during the 1812 and 1849 Seminole Wars.

As interesting as this history is, it was never taught in the Wewoka school system. Sadly, I would not learn of it until some 20 years later after graduating high school in 1993. By then, I was incarcerated in one of

California's maximum security housing units. Learning of all this unquestionably gave me a sense of pride in such a dark place. I was from the small town called "barking water", which was the Seminole-Gullah translation of Wewoka.

At the same time there was the anger and the frustration knowing that there were those who referred to it as "Coon Creek". These were those who strove to obliterate from the pages of history the fact that it was my family, my ancestors—the Caesar Bruner Band of Black Seminoles—that founded this township long before Oklahoma became a state in 1907. They were the ones who, to this day, strive to strip Wewoka of her crown as the county seat of Seminole County. They are the ones that worked tirelessly to deprive it of economic opportunities and culturally centered education. They are the ones that exploited the poverty and criminal culture that sprung from the social political structures and conditions they created that influenced kids like me who became dope dealers, killers, pimps and thieves in order to survive.

Yes, the Wewoka I grew up in was plagued with more than its share of inner-city problems. There were limited job opportunities: two grocery stores, a handful of family-owned convenience stores, several nursing homes, a feed store, General Dollar Store, Family Dollar, a few mechanic and muffler shops, and your run-of-the-mill of entrepreneurs and law enforcement agencies: BIA, the courthouse and the District Attorney's Office. Each had its token Negro and Native. The rest of us had our nickel-and-dime hustles: selling produce from home grown gardens, mowing lawns, plowing gardens, bootlegging, pimping, boosting, drug-dealing, etc.

Growing up, I had a front-row seat to them all. My Grandpa Willis was a hustler of the sorts. Both he and my Grandma Jean kept me with my hands in the dirt grinding produce and mowing lawns as a kid. Grandpa was born to a black father and Native American mother in Konawa. It was another one of those small towns in Seminole County, like Wewoka, that had its own history of racism too.

His mother, he always told me as a child, had disowned him due to the black blood that ran through his veins. Growing up, I could tell this deeply pained him so. From time to time he would speak about it. His chin would drop to his chest and his eyes would fill with pain as they roamed the ground beneath him in search of his dignity. "I grew up with my cousin James... He and I were raised by my grandmother. My mother didn't want anything to do with me...." he would utter with such sadness. His soul had been so tainted by racism that the pain it caused would ultimately drive him to find peace of mind at the bottom of a bottle. It also made him distrustful of the white man. "You can love them. You can be friends with them. But you better not ever trust them," he would always warn me.

My grandmother was completely opposite in terms of racism's affect. She was the Dr. Martin Luther King type who judged people based on their character. Where my grandfather rejected much of the white world, my grandmother played her role in it and accepted it. She was the servant who served both black and white world's alike as a housekeeper, in-house nurse and advocate. Although my grandmother's character was dignified and just, I believe racism's subversive and explicit effect led her to believe that white was in fact "better" and in proving so, she gave her first child up for adoption because of her skin tone, which was darker than night. Eventually, she had two more biracial children by white men—my mother who everyone affectionately called Sticky and my Uncle Dekoven, who she raised and would put her all into. Still and yet she too would attempt to find peace at the bottom of a bottle.

Despite my grandparents' issues, they were the world to me. Ever since I could remember, they dotted on me with love and affection. They provided me the attention and affection much needed for a healthy childhood and taught me so much. Our favorite pastime? Fishing. As a boy I would grow up in my grandfather's apprenticeship. Not only did he teach me how to fish, there were the lessons in character, self-reliance, and God. Of course, there was the mischief as well.

When I was a child, my cousin Elrather and I would often stray off from church on Sunday afternoons into the surrounding wilderness. We were adventurous boys. One day time quickly got away from us and before we realized it, we had strayed off some five or six miles from the church. There we where, knee deep in a clear-water pond trying to catch some fish with our bare hands. Fortunately, the pond was within view of the road and in the direction our grandparents had to travel to return home.

Looking back I can only imagine the frustration and worry that struck our grandparents when they discovered we were no longer to be found on the church grounds. But then, knowing my grandfather, he was probably like, "Those goddamn boys. Let them find their own way home!" Though his frustration would soon be realized once they laid eyes on us. Boy did we get a lashing. Not only had we wondered off from church, but we had ruined our church clothes.

After that my grandmother made a deal with us. She was always the peacekeeper. If we agreed to attend Sunday school and stayed out of trouble, she would agree to take us to the local swimming pool and ice cream parlor every Sunday after church. It would not take much convincing. Thereafter, we became angels on Sundays and mischievous little devils Monday through Saturday.

My grandparents were the best. They invested so much in us as human beings. At this time, it was still an era of "yes ma'am" and "no sir" and so manners and respect for others were priority on their list of lessons.

Since becoming church folks they had exchanged the bottle for the Bible and Jesus. So many fond memories so many stories I could tell about them. They were my rock to say the least in a nutshell.

As for my mother, the most fondest memory of her was she and I eating oysters and her taking me to the annual Wewoka Fair. I recall being as young as four or five years old and impatiently waiting as she stood at the kitchen counter with a can opener and manually opened a small can of seafood. She would then drench them in Tabasco sauce and take delight. Of course, sharing them was not part of the plan. That's why the hot sauce. Guess she thought it would deter me from enjoying the little delicacies she could not afford but every so often. Not! I would ask and she would kindly respond with mischief in her soft southern voice, "Son... They are hot and will burn your little tough." She would smile knowing I was stubborn enough to taste the flame. Off I would go screaming and running through the house tongue burning like hot wheels on a drag car as my little hands fanned my mouth for comfort.

The annual fair was any kids favorite, especially mine. For me it was a special time of the year that my mother and I would bond and spend some quality time together outside of the norm of family life. Looking back over the years, I realize it was an escape. For her those times were the only time life seemed normal and she would have some aspect of normalcy. For the complications of mental illness and addiction were compiling daily. She would see the opportunity to be a kid again herself as she and I would take to the lines of every ride like kids in a candy store. I would play the mini carnival games and often walk away with a small prize, a cheap poster or stuffed animal or toy of some sort to give to my Queen. Where she would find money for us to enjoy this past time was beyond me. But then most kids did not think of these things. But I was not most kids.

Tragedy would strike when I was three years old. My father would be shot dead, leaving my mother devastated. As can be expected, this would have a major impact on me as a child as well. Today, I look back and I vividly recall the kid cowboy I aspired to be. It was a child's attempt to carry on with his father's influence. Even more, and it would take me years before I realized this, but I had also been influenced by my father's fighting spirit. However, where he was said to be a brawler, I was stubborn as a mule and, once my heels dug in, in for the good fight.

Often I have wondered what life would have been like if I had my father to carry me throughout my youth into my adulthood. When I look to his brothers, my uncles, I see the stability they provided their children, most of which have gone on to live productive lives. Not having this stability unquestionably invited chaos into my mother and my lives.

Often the electricity was shut off at a home because there was addiction and money was spent on getting high. Yet somehow, moms managed to keep us healthy and fed. She was a nurse and there was always a pot of red beans and rice on the stove. Surprisingly, after all these years in prison, beans and rice are all I can enjoy.

Still and yet, when it was time for the fair, moms and I would be front and center of the action. She dressed up in her new Dollar General Store outfit, a cheap jogging suit and a pair of Payless shoes with a Kool filter King menthol cigarette hanging from her mouth to give me the best few days a kid could ask for. Boy it felt good. For a few days I was special with a cool mom. These were the days. Life was simple and I was well... No... no I was not innocent.

I was a mannish kid. Around seven or eight years old I discovered my baby sitter's girl parts and quickly learned "The Milk Bar" was open for the green eyed monster, me! The honey pot was for boys to take delight in. Simply put, titties were toys to me as a kid and I loved playing with them. Of all the kinkiest things a kid could do, my moms would tell me that, as a child, I had this thing for burying my face in one of her girlfriend's behind or crotch. I would take a good sniff exhale and be like, "Robin your pussy stank!" For years thereafter every time I would see her the running joke was, "Robin gone with your stank ass booty!" We would bust up laughing, remembering that innocent boy who would speak so bluntly.

***

The murder of my father, my mother's mental illness and drug addiction, and, later, my grandparents growing infirm, would force me to grow up fast. These events affected me in such a way that my innocence as a child would be completely shattered; leaving little, if any, figment of an ordinary childhood.

Consequently, I would learn early on in life the tragedies we are bound to face from the Cradle to the Grave. This, in turn, would shape both my emotional and social independence. In time, I would mature. The mannish boy would quickly grow into a reserved man. And yet, before he could accomplish anything, there was the instability, impulsiveness and lack of self-esteem he would have to encounter and conquer.

School Days

At the center of every story I write there is always Cedar Street. Every small town, big city or outback country dirt patch has its urban center, its segregated Mecca of ill repute. Wewoka was no different. Cedar Street was our university. It was the place where we learned about whose mother was a "strawberry" and we learned the gambles in life: trappin', pimping, how to shoot craps, and bootlegging.

It was our county commercial center for black entertainment. A sort of BET for country folk.

As a kid, I would spend a considerable amount of time on Cedar Street. As if yesterday, I recall the small row of shotgun houses and red brick mortar buildings that lined the block. Clyde's Barber Shop, Bertha's Hair Salon, Momma Dolly's Juke Joint, and a few other establishments kept a steady flow of foot traffic, day or night. My grandparents often frequented these establishments with me in tow to socialize with friends and, of course, play a game of chance.

Often, we would visit with Cousin Tobie or Willie Moe who were my grandparents' closest friends. Both men were bootleggers. So it came as no surprise that my grandparents spent a many a day sitting on a stump in front of their shotgun shack with a mason jar full of corn whiskey and a bushel of wild onions and fresh caught catfish.

Willie Moe was a quiet man, standing around six foot three with a slender build. A man of prudence, he was a simple man, gracious and ever one to accommodate you with a two dollar jar of "fire water" and a good conversation.

Cousin Tobie, on the other hand, was a dandy. Well groomed with a midsize build, he fancied himself as a hustler of the sorts. In addition to being your "half pint" man after the liquor store closed, he would accommodate you to any destination within reason for a small fee. Next to Willie Moe, he was one of my most fondest of people growing up. As a child, he would often taught me with a knife, "I'm going to cut your little badass mothafucka," he would threaten playfully before reaching into his pocket to produce a glistening blade. In time I would grow to reciprocate the taunts. I kept a knife too; mostly for cleaning fish and handiwork.

Looking back, Cedar Street was for me a university of life lessons. There, on this small town street, lined with shotgun houses and red big brick buildings, a tight-knit community thrived. At its heart, was Nobletown Elementary and Douglas High School. Next to our family, our schools are the primary agent of socialization. In them, we learn certain values affecting our behaviors. Without question, they play a significant role in our character development. We learn, for example, the rules of social engagement with our peers and others. Ultimately, we learn to accept or reject certain norms within society.

I vividly recall those formal years of my education. Nobletown was a product of Jim Crow segregation. In 1979, when I started kindergarten, Nobletown was an all black school with all black teachers. It was the cornerstone to black progress in Seminole County. At the helm, stood Richard Carolina. A posed man, Principal Carolina was a man of vision; actively involved in not only the school but the community. He came from a hard-working, patriotic African American family who strove to make the black educational experience meaningful. His nephews, Andre and Robert, were my childhood friends. There were many days that we would spend popping wheelies on our bikes and fighting as kids.

There, at Nobletown, I would be shielded from the racism I would later to experience at Wewoka Elementary after graduating to first grade. Why my mother had opted to send me there I do not know. But the transfer would be an adjustment to say the least. In fact, this would be an understatement. I would go from an all-black school to one staff by all white people, racist white people. With the exception of a few token black teachers, my new school was whiter than a snow-capped mountain in Tahoe.

Going into this environment would be traumatic. The reality being, I went from a community of teachers with the stake in my future to one where the teachers hated my very being. To this day, I still feel the shame, the insecurity of being black that they would instill in me. As a kid, I would attempt to defend my ego by playing up to the fact that I had white blood running through my veins just to make my white peers feel comfortable playing with me. In time, I would learn that my only reprieve from this was sticking to my own kind and rebellion!

Indeed, I would grow to be a rebellious kid who early on caught the vapors of racism that heavily dominated and influenced the pulse of my education and what I was to experience as a failing student and artist. A gifted artist, my art, like my antics, was created to inspire two things: humor and rebellion. The latter, I accomplished by simply refusing to do my school work and instead doodled on any and every surface that served as a canvas.

Of course, none of this was in vain. My rejection of my white teachers' idea of "education" in time would preserve my self-esteem and create within me a keen ability to look beyond many of the ideals forced upon me by white society. This would later in life inspire me to think outside the box when faced with a life sentence in prison. And so the journey began.

Trappin'

As early as I can remember, I had this ability to look beyond the surface of my surroundings and seek deeper meaning and understanding of the events that played out before me. In time, this would possess me with an astute ability to observe people, places and things—life in general. I noted both strengths and weaknesses, even within myself. I was and remain my biggest critic, teacher and disciplinarian.

Growing up, one of the first of many observations I would make of my mother was her gift of gab. Man!, could that woman talk a good game. Highly intelligent, moms could easily convince you to buy into her dream, business and or struggle. If it was a business plan, she would easily convince you to fund it. If it was a matter of putting food on the table or paying the bills, she could articulate the struggle in such a way that you were instantly struck with a bleeding heart. And when that failed, off to Dan's Pawn Shop we went.

I remember those trips to the pawn shop being in essence a 101: Guide How to Debate for Dummies. When Mom's options tapped out, off she went to Dan's with our TV, or anything else of value we had, which was not much. There, I would stand guard on the tips of my toes, leaning on his checkout counter to observe their exchange. Mom would state her position. Dan would counter. Mom would counter with another offer, then hold firm knowing his profit margins. She never settled for anything less than her bottom line. Why it was she always made it a point for me to be present? I can only assume it was because she wanted to teach me a lesson about life, struggle.

Indeed, from struggle came hustle. And everybody in the neighborhood had to have one. Necessity knew no law. So we learned not to judge people for doing what they had to do in order to survive. Consequently, to be a hustler, this taught me early on in life to have a certain level of respect and appreciation for the grind; to be creative and, most importantly, persevere.

Struggle taught me the value of a dollar. And rule of thumb was, never spend one unless you have 10 more coming in. Of course, saving and investing were also part of the equation. As a kid, I saved every penny, nickel and dime I got my hand on. Money, I quickly learned, equated to security and freedom. And so I learned to keep my piggy bank hidden from my broke ass mother. This, in turn taught me that, when it came to your money, it was best to play broke and look broke.

My grandparents taught me well. Both my mother and father's parents were conservative folk. They only bought what they needed and used their credit for business purposes. Never was there a time or occasion that I can honestly recall them splurging. Despite being financially stable, they never bought a new car or clothes, went on vacation or spent money frivolously on cosmetics. In fact, I can honestly say that, during my lifetime, my dad's father only owned two vehicles: an old Ford truck and my father's 1964 Impala. Both my grandpa Willis and he wore coveralls seven days a week. Now, of course, my grandparents had their Sunday attire they would don for church or a funeral.

Naturally, it would take me years to master my insecurities. During my teens and early twenties, they would get the best of me. I had got caught up in the culture of Hip Hop. Flashy, I would come into money and splurge on cars, clothes and jewelry. Just as any kid, I had to learn the lessons of money. Fortunately, I had enough hustle to keep a dollar or two coming in here and there.

When it came to my hustle, my grandparents Jean and Willis would instill in me a certain level of discipline that would carry on with me to this day. As young as five or six years of age, our grandparents would encourage Elrather and I to collect bottles and cans. We would fill the entire bed of a pickup truck within a month, then take that trip to the recycle company to cash in.

During this time, we would spend our evenings with Grandpa plowing and seeding a garden. After some 20 years in prison, I can still smell the fresh plowed dirt and remember its cool feel on my hands as I often suck them into the soil to birth a seed. Watching that seed grow in rich, fertilized soil would teach me in time the process by which life, or even success for that much, took its course: we have to cultivate our soil (I.e., our unconscious input), plant our seeds (I.e., ideas), and then nurture them with our efforts so as to reap the benefits of our labor.

When we were not collecting cans and bottles or seeding a garden, my grandfather had us working as partners in a small landscaping company he had started. We would awake at dawn, load our equipment and head out for a day's work. It was an intense, hard labor, that at 10 years of age, shaped my ability to persevere for it allowed a rewarding experience: stay the course despite obstacle, mental or physical exhaustion. Indeed, those were some long, hot yet paid summer days that rewarded me with both character and a few dollars in my pocket.

By the time I was 13 years old, I had pretty much settled in my ways. I had observed the best and worst of the world before me and, despite all the positive lessons, I was gradually drifting into darkness and chaos.

* * *

1987: Crack-cocaine hit Wewoka hard. The first crack house popped up on the corner of Eufaula and 4th Street. Preston Reese was a fair complexioned man well into his fifties. During the summer months, he hustled fresh caught catfish. On any given day, you could find him and his crew neck deep in a river noodling. More hustle than sport, they would always return with today's catch stored in a deep freezer outfitted on the back of his pickup truck with a gas generator. From one town to the next they would travel throughout the county selling fish and crack cocaine.

Preston's crack house on Eufaula Street was where I would first get introduced to the notion of selling crack. One day, Andrae, a childhood friend, approached me with a proposal: "I know where we can make $40 a night." Me being game for a hustle, I was in without even a question. And so the story goes... Thereafter, Dre and I would spend our weekends during the summer of 1987 trapping as lookouts behind a fortified door at Preston's crack house. Occasionally, we would get the opportunity to make a few extra dollars dispensing $20 hubbas (crack rocks) to the neighborhood dope fiends. Instantly, a seed was planted!

Before long, I was getting fronted small amounts of crack cocaine, then purchasing double ups and flipping my money on Cedar Street. By now Willie Moe had passed away and his shack had been demolished along with the other structures that once lined the block. Pooches, which was a two-bedroom house that had been relocated and converted into a juke joint, now stood as a trap house (dope house). There, I would begin learning the tricks of the trade: security, manufacturing, marketing and promotion, and, most important, the treacherous slope I was now trekking upon.

Of all my lessons and teachers, my cousin Regina would be instrumental in teaching me just how shady the streets were. She stood 5'8" and was brown skinned with a shapely figure. I remember often traveling to Oklahoma City to visit her and her mother, my Aunt Betty, as a kid. It would be a reunion for her and my mother who both grew up together. Regina had grew up in both Wewoka and the Eastside of Oklahoma City. A fast talker, and a beautiful brown skin, she, very much like my mother, could talk a cat off the back of a fish truck. And like my mother, she too struggled with addiction.

Regina was what we called on the streets a runner, someone who would refer crack customers for a small fee, usually in exchange for drugs. But because I would not sell her dope, she settled for money, which I knew she would smoke up anyway. But at least it was not on my conscience. Despite this, she was definitely good for bringing me a few hundred dollars a night which for me at the time was good money. Usually after a good night, her slick ass would run a con on me. She ran so many con games on me that by the time she was done, I could have wrote Biggie Smalls' 10 Crack Commandments:

1. Never let no one know how much dough you hold.
2. Never let 'em know your next move.
3. Never trust nobody.
4. Never get high, on your own supply.
5. Never sell no crack where you rest at.
6. That goddamn credit? Dead it. Money up front.
7. Keep your family and business completely separated.
8. Never keep no weight on you.
9. If you ain't gettin bags stay the fuck from police.
10. A strong word called consignment; if you ain't got the clientele say hell no.

Number One would eventually lead to a wedge being driven between several friends and I. It began to develop during our childhood. They would barrage me with comments like "You're spoiled" or "Pretty boy". They would say these things because I always had money to buy toys, bikes or the latest gear. Where my grandparents taught me the concept of the "fruits of my labor", they had yet to learn these valuable lessons.

As we grew older and took to the streets, the envy became more intense. At first I did not recognize the signs. I thought we were friends. But then they would make subtle comments like, "Man!, how you got two Chevy's and I ain't got car the one!?!" Or "Man, why you ain't putting Niggas on?" (Little did they realize I was taking losses putting broke niggas on.)

Undoubtedly, these would be some very trying times. I was young, impressionable, and like any kid, I sought acceptance by trying to prove them wrong. I was not spoiled or a pretty boy! And yet, the harder I tried to convince them or the more people that I "put on" or extended myself to, the more they grew to despise me. Eventually, as I'm to detail in the coming pages, all this would lead to me killing my best friend.

California Dreaming

December 1994, the 20 year old kid stood at the register in Church's Chicken in Tulsa, Oklahoma. I was preparing to board a Greyhound bus for a two-day ride to California and wanted to grab something to eat before departing. It had been some seven years since I had seen my Grandpa Willis and some ten years since seeing Elrather. When I was around 13 years old, my grandparents had began to grow infirm. Eventually, their health complications would result in them being separated. Grandpa was to move to California with his daughter, my Aunt Beverly who was Elrather's mother. My Grandma Jean, unfortunately, was admitted to a nursing home on account of her Alzheimer's requiring 24 hour around the clock observation.

When Elrather was about nine years old he had moved to California as well to live with his mother. By December 1994, he had become somewhat a fixture in the Bay Area. He had lived in all the trap spots: East Oakland, North Richmond, Hunters Point in San Francisco, Crestside in Vallejo, and the El Pueblo Projects in Pittsburg.

I would board the Greyhound bus that evening with a bucket of chicken and about $15k in trap money. My tapered Afro was on point. I wore a blue Notre Dame pullover sweater and my Dickies were freshly creased. The Nike Cortez on my feet were brand new. I was on the come up.

On any given day, I had a team of 20 or better soliders in the streets who stood beside me. We were a click of Crips, Bloods and hustlers. I needed a plug on the *work* (I.e., a kilogram of crack cocaine) so I could feed the block. Elrather, who everyone now called Ray, was to make the introductions and I would take it from there.

Two days later, the Greyhound docked in San Jose, California—the East Bay Area. Ray was waiting outside in an old, beat-up 1974 Cutlass. When I stepped out onto the sidewalk and looked up at the buildings, I recall vividly how they seemed to extend into the sky without limit. At that moment I was overwhelmed with a profound sense of the possibilities that lay before me. The world suddenly changed. My newborn daughter was three weeks old and I realized in that moment California was a place I could build my dreams and dream big. It was a place where dreams became realities.

Seeing my grandfather after all those years was a bit touching to say the least. He was still the fiery old man he had always been. Shortly after I had arrived, he let it be known how much he disliked living in California; how, when he was in the Navy and stationed at Port

Chicago, he was more than happy to get the hell out of the state. "Take me home! I don't like this city shit. I'm a country boy!" he plead.

Yet for the best of me, I could not wrap my mind around what about the city he could not possibly love. I was so caught up in the novelty of it that I simply failed to comprehend that life in the city was not as simple as it was back home. Personally, seeing the big city lights and the hustle and bustle of life in the Bay, was exactly the type of place I wanted to be. Yet my grandfather simply craved the peace of mind he had left back home in Oklahoma.

He missed those days of sitting on his porch and watching his cattle graze in the fields. Most of all, and it would take me years before I realized this, he missed the people. We came from a place where people knew their neighbors and their friends for a lifetime. Good old Southern hospitality. California, I would learn, was much different. People really did not concern themselves with their neighbors affairs and the density of the Metropolitan City made it difficult to develop lasting friendships.

For the next two weeks Ray would take me on a tour around the Bay Area. We hit every hip hop club and trap spot in the East Bay. It was simply amazing all the different ethnicities of people that gave California its vibe. There were Ethiopians, Arabians, Latinos, Colombians, Asians—each having their own distinct community and culture. And the women! Not that Oklahoma did not have its share of beautiful women. But it was something about those Cali girls that made a cowboy chaff in the pants. They were exotic, independent and simply beautiful. I was lost in the big city lights.

While in California, I marveled at the possibilities that I was being exposed to. It was unlike anything I had seen or experienced back home. The Bay was exuberant, flashy and buzzing with activity 24 hours around the clock. And there I was as country as Hee Haw. I decided right then and there I was going to be moving to the West Coast soon.

Looking back, it is difficult for me to explain why I did not return with my grandfather. Instead, I returned with 2.205 pounds of powder cocaine. Here, the internal conflicts began. The idea of escaping Oklahoma tore at the fabric of my ambition and clashed with the responsibility of being the head of my family and neighborhood. Then too, I was soon to learn there were some obstacles I would have to face in light of my recent fortune.

Little did I realize then, but I had begin to outgrow my surroundings. My ambitions were too Hollywood for a small town. Yet I felt trapped in a cultural bubble that would not allow for me to reach for the possible. I was determined to escape the monotony of the simple life. Unknowingly, I would not have but 11 months on the streets before I would be arrested and charged with capital murder.

Death By Lethal Injection

March 3rd 2003, I was set to begin my trial for first-degree murder at the Alameda County Courthouse in Oakland, California. As I sat in the courtroom over the course of the next few weeks, I was often visited by this overwhelming sense of despair. How could this have happened? How is it that I found myself *again* charged with capital murder? This would be the second time I found myself facing these charges. I could not believe it.

Another life gone. Two black men destined to meet their fate from a series of events that would cumulate in the physical death of one and the social death of the other. Whereas, one was shot, killed, and left to die on a West Oakland ghetto street corner, and the other bound to the California Department of Corrections and [r]ehabilitation to begin a life sentence without the possibility of parole. And so the story begins.

November 1998, I arrived in Pittsburg, California after a 24-hour cross country drive with my younger sister Gwendolyn and my uncle Victor. He had offered to drive us to our grandfather's (his father). The plan was I would get a new start on life there after I was released from prison. I was 24 years old. Gwen was 18 and unbeknownst to us all, pregnant with her first child. The drive was scenic to say the least after having spent the past three years in a backwoods county jail and prison cell. It was day number ten after being discharged from the Cimarron City Correctional Facility in Cushing, Oklahoma. In the wee hours of the morning we departed from the small town of Seminole after loading up in my uncle's 1993 S10 Chevrolet pick-up truck and heading west to the Bay Area. As we drove down Interstate 40, I thought about how I had just spent the past thirty-six months *literally* fighting for my life and I somehow miraculously came out victorious. It was a humbling experience no doubt.

November 25, 1995, I remember waking up that morning and feeling unprepared for what lay ahead. You can never forget a day like this, because unfortunately it was the day that I attended a friend's funeral. Something in my gut had been eating at me and it did not help the situation that my home had been burglarized the week before. My family and I were not safe. We had been violated, and unbeknownst to us all, we were about to find out that it was a close friend who had shattered our sense of security.

It was a gangster's funeral, so I dressed accordingly: a new pair of black oversized Dickies pants, a new black Nike pullover sweater, and a matching pair of black Nike Cortez with the white swoosh sign. After getting dressed, I picked out my Afro, rolled up a few blunts for the trip, and grabbed my chrome plated Tech-9 and two extra clips. My baby mama cooked breakfast.

We ate in silence before hopping into my newly restored 1971 four door Chevy Caprice to take the dreaded hour drive from Bristow to Wewoka.

When we arrived, I would walk into a funeral gathering expecting to pay my respects to the deceased, Desi Khamis Nash, a.k.a Khamis, a distant relative. But I was only to emerge from a frenzy of screaming onlookers as I had just shot and killed my best friend, Conan Emery. Just like that, in a flash of gunfire and the quickness of a trigger pulled, he was dead and my entire life was turned upside down. Everything, and *I mean everything,* that I believed up until that point in my life would eventually come crashing down on my shoulders. The circumstances and my so-called friend's betrayal and treachery would force me to reckon with the life that I was living. Paying my respects would not be in the cards this day as I was about to learn that many of my former friendships and affiliations would come to an abrupt end.

Thereafter, for years to come, I would often replay the events that led up to this tragedy, trying to make sense of it. In the weeks prior to his murder,

Khamis had just been released from the California Youth Authority. He was 17 years old, penitentiary built, and an active gang member. Like many kids his age, he was turned-up and eager to prove himself. About a week before he was killed, he and I were sitting in my car in the parking lot outside of Bubbas and Eric Williams' game room. We were making small talk about "the plan", that is, what he was planning to do with his life now that he had returned home from California. I remember him lighting up at the sight of a chrome plated 357 Magnum I had sitting under my arm rest. I was heavy in the dope game at the time and had it for protection. That's when he started talking about banging (representing) Crip.

Jermaine and Khamis had recently had a run-in with Derrick Jackson, a young kid from New Lima, a small suburb outside of Wewoka. Derrick, a.k.a. "Set Trip", was about the same age as Khamis. He claimed to be a blood gang member. I had known him since he was a kid as well. He was five years younger than me and I had watched him grow up during my school years at New Lima; I knew his family too. His cousins and uncles were known brawlers and hustlers around Seminole County and his mother and aunts often partied with my mom.

Not one to turn down a fade (fight), Derrick fought hard like his life and reputation depended on every blow. He never backed down and often, when in Wewoka, found himself out numbered by Crips. I knew from watching him go toe-to-toe with almost every Crip in the 'hood, it was only a matter of time before he leveled the playing field by picking up a pistol. Realizing this, and the fact that he was a country boy like myself who loved to play with guns, I attempted to encourage both Khamis and Jermaine, who at the time were around 16 or 17 years old, to focus on getting money and to leave Derrick alone.

Within a week or so, Khamis would be dead, shot twice in the chest after Jermaine and he chased Derrick down in a high-speed car chase. When the cars came to a stop, Derrick hung out the window and shot twice just as Khamis and Jermaine jumped from the jeep they were in and banged Crip. It would be the last time he threw up the set. Derrick would clap back with a 22 caliber revolver, leaving Khamis to die as his lungs filled with blood.

Thereafter, Jermaine would inform the police that Derrick was the shooter. After Derrick was arrested and thrown in jail, Jermaine would testify at Derrick's preliminary hearing. After the shooting, Jermaine's brother Jamerl would call me to inform of the murder. I recall driving down to Seminole to speak with them about it with a heavy heart. That was when Jermaine and I clashed. After informing me of the fact that he had ratted Derrick out, Jermaine had the audacity to ask me for a gun so he could retaliate. I must have looked at him like he was a God damned fool to think that I was about to give him a gun after he had just snitched on somebody.

What happened after that disagreement would be pure speculation, but I surmise that Jermaine would appeal to Conan his sentiment that I was a "sucker," and that I wouldn't give him a strap to retaliate (of course leaving out the details of why), and that my apparent lack of commitment to the "set" needed to be dealt with. Conan's actions would validate my suspicions,

Jermaine and he would burglarize my home, making off with several guns along with a few other items.

It was now time for me to break ties with the set. Conan had violated me and bit the hand that fed him. And all but two of my so-called "gangster ass" homeboys would walk into the courtroom a couple years later with Dickies sagging and tell an all-white jury that, at that moment, when it all jumped off, "Ivan stepped to the side of the couch that Conan was sitting on, pulled out a chrome Tech-9, racked it and shot him point-blank in the head." Twelve jurors, twelve "yeses" to lethally inject me upon a finding of guilt. I watched in pain and disbelief as one witness after another, one gang banger after another, testified against me.

Of them all, the one testimony I will never forget was that of my so-called "God brother" Gerald Gordan, a.k.a. Peanut. Peanut stood about six feet two inches tall and had a fair complexion, he often stuttered when he spoke. We had known each other since we were children. As teenagers, we partied and stole cars together, shoplifted from the local thrift stores, and spent many summer nights and days walking the streets of Wewoka with our homeboys looking for some mischief to get into. At the time, he claimed to be a member of the Hoover Crip gang. But as he sat on that stand and sung like a canary, I could not help but feel sorry for him. "I want to kill him," Peanut testified in reference to me. "But the state is going to give him the death penalty. So I'll let them do it!"

I felt sorry for him as I watched in silence as he sat in the courtroom and signified with all the courage of a king's jester his regard to see me lethally injected. Blunt, Yogi, Sidney, Jermaine, Jamerl, and Conan's brother, Cameron—all claiming to be gangsters—would follow suit. It was at that point of my life that I realized my so-called "homeboys" were not about that street life. They stood before a jury and testified against me, and did so in face of the fact that they all knew Conan had struck the first blow when he broke into my family's home and later let it be known "fuck me" — all of which was a true testament to their shifty ass character and a major contradiction of the street code we all proclaimed to live by.

I knew right then and there that being part of the street gang culture was not for me. I had been loyal to the set; fed niggas; invited them into my home and treated them like family, only to have my hand bitten. It was time for me to recognize the "real." The real being what my mother had always said about my so-called friends, "They don't give a fuck about you... They don't give a fuck about your newborn baby... They don't give a fuck about your family... They don't give a fuck about your well-being in face of Conan's actions... They simply don't give a fuck!"

Fortunately, the jury never arrived at a guilty verdict. Hung 9 to 3, in favor to acquit in self-defense, I would spend a total of 36 months of my life caged like an animal. After accepting a deal for four years with time served, I made the second biggest mistake of my life. Accepting that plea bargain made me another statistic, another black kid with a felony record.

***

People often ask me how is it that I have twice stood before a jury charged with murder and seemingly did not learn my lesson? Obviously, the question assumes a lot and fails to take into account the circumstances that prompt one to kill. Yes, unfortunately I have killed twice. And unlikely as it may seem, I did so in self-defense.

Here, I often explain to people that the reality that brought me to such a point in my life was largely due to my failure to recognize how I had allowed myself, as my aunt would eventually say, "…to be around people I would have to hurt." In a nutshell, I created life-threatening circumstances due to my activities and association with certain characters.

My belief system also played a significant role. Like many young black men caught up in the streets, I adopted the creed "kill or be killed". Even more, I ignored the warning signs displayed by my so-called friends' betrayal and treachery. So it's not that I did not learn something from my first murder trial, or even the second. Facing execution at age 21 by lethal injection definitely taught me a lesson or two. Namely, I came away with a newfound sense of confidence that would allow me to conquer my fears no matter how life-threatening they were.

Schoolboy

After paroling from prison in Oklahoma, ten days later I would move to California. I began to realize I could no longer afford to be a reaction. It was time to grow the fuck up and get that grown man money. So I figured a good place to start was college. Two months after leaving Oklahoma, I was a full time college student with a backpack, sandals and a library card. At 24 years old, this was a major transitional period where the events of life temporarily pushed me in a new direction, away from the streets and into a new city and new setting I would have to learn how to navigate quickly. It was a time to learn, to learn how to think methodically, technically and more importantly, logically.

The irony of walking onto a college campus as a student after having been acquitted in a capital murder trial and discharging a prison sentence was a given. I was audacious, going from one extreme to another, from one institution to the other. Little did I realize at the time the same people who ran the prison system also ran the nation's educational system. Still and yet, I pushed forward. And every step, every day and every breath I took would be met with a challenge.

Never had I felt so out of place as I did the day I walked onto the campus at Los Medanos Community College in Pittsburg, California. Doubt shadowed my every move as I struggled with insecurity. I was not exactly what you call schoolboy material. I was a former crack dealer and, arguably, a murderer. I had been convicted of manslaughter and now sat amongst a bunch of kids and professors who I would imagine had never seen the inside of a prison cell. Let alone stood before a jury on a capital murder charge. Where most of these kids carried books and backpacks, I carried a 13 shot 45 cal. llama pistol. Naturally, all this weighed heavily on my conscience like an oxygen tank. I could not breathe without inhaling a sense of being an imposter.

One day, I recall I was sitting in on a lecture presentation for my business law class when the professor began a discussion about the different statues and penal codes for civil law. Eventually the focus of the conversation between the professor and class somehow turned on trials and criminal proceedings. Instantly, my mind began to play tricks on me as if an old Geto Boys' song. Paranoid, I begin to think someone in the room had known my secret and had intentionally stirred the conversation in this direction in an effort to expose me. I looked about the class frantically and yet it seemed the only thing that was out of place was me. So I got up and I left with intentions of never coming back.

Still, I showed up the next day and the next willing to give change a chance. After going through everything that happened in Oklahoma, I was motivated to change. Like most people, who had to be motivated by an external force, I was no different. Be it to change to become a better person, give up an addiction of some sort or simply to attend college, we needed a driving force (I.e., a source of encouragement or support behind us to take a step in a different direction). Looking back today, I now see how those events in Oklahoma were indeed external forces that compelled me to take a serious look at life and push forward onto uncharted waters.

Transition, however, would not come easy. Realistically, I could not be thought to so easily shed my old skin. First, I would have to grow a new one. In the meantime I had to survive. The scales of my old lifestyle—that I was desperately attempting to shed— had provided protection and nourishment. College was not paying the rent. Nor were any of the odd jobs I worked. And the Bay Area was one of the most expensive places in the United States to live. So there I was once again on campus grinding dime bags of weed. I was getting it the best way I knew how. Thinking that if I stayed off the block and stayed away from the hard stuff (I.e., crack cocaine), then I would avoid the drama and riff raff that came along with the grind. WRONG AGAIN!"

At first things were smooth. I collected chips from a small clientele there at the LMC. On the weekends, Ray and I would jump on the Amtrak train and travel to Fresno where we were able to quickly build a clientele at Fresno State University. Over the years we had managed to stay in touch. When I finally moved to California, he would greatly assist me to get back on my feet and introduced me to his circle and a childhood friend of his named Charlie who played football at the university. As it turned out Fresno State would be a goldmine! We would jump off the train with a few pounds of sticky icky and within a couple of hours— dime bags, eighths, ounces—it would all be gone!

By the end of the summer of 1999 I had a steady flow of clients and had decided to move from Pittsburg to Oakland. Oakland was a 45-minute train ride from Los Medonos. It feel good moving into my own place after having spent the first eight months or so living with my aunt after I had discharged from Cushing. It was a small studio located within a short distance of the downtown area.

During the summer I had worked a construction gig to renovate the apartment complex and, after establishing a good rapport with the owner, was able to get the place at a reduced rate in exchange for doing some managerial work.

A few weeks in, I quickly came to realize I was sitting in the midst of a trap spot. Telegraph & Sycamore was located next to 2-4, notorious heroin spot that extended into deep West Oakland. Every day I would post up at the site and watch the foot traffic come in droves to frequent a gang the trap stars who were running a trap out of the neighboring apartment complex. It was major! A million-dollar operation, the block never slept. People came and went at all times of the day and night. And I was not the only one watching.

By the time November '99 rolled around the Feds was serving indictments. Instantly, the block became a ghost town. All the trap stars, with the exception of a few, had been arrested. And the turf was now wide open for the taking. Me being hustler, I had established myself with a few of the local business owners who occasionally dipped and dabbed and some of my product. After the Feds cleared out I instantly went to work setting up shop. Overnight, I went from selling a few bags of weed to selling pounds. Things eventually grew to a point where I had to put together a three-man crew to dispense product day and night.

One of my up and coming protégés was a young 18 year old kid named AG, whose father I had worked with in construction. AG knew his way around the Bay Area and had a small clientele that spanned from Pittsburg to San Francisco. On an average he would come through and buy a few ounces a week to get his lunch money. He was a bright kid who hustled hard and reminded me of myself when I was his age. For the most part he had his head on his shoulders straight and was planning to attend college in Kentucky after graduating high school. Though, as to be expected, he was a little green when it came to staying sucka free. Here is where shit would go left.

If it was one thing I had learned from the relationship and tragedy with Conan, it was, there is no honor amongst thieves. Today, I often tell people that, if you find yourself in the midst of a friend who will steal from a friend, it's a given that that friend will also steal from you.

AG, being young and a bit naïve when it came to the streets, had took to hanging out with a crew of stick-up kids. Like most, they robbed at gunpoint partygoers, corner hustlers, or any mark they could find. From jump, I let AG know that what these youngsters were doing did not mix with what we had going on. I then told him to keep lil' Will (aka William Anderson), who was the ringleader, out of our mix. But it was too late.

July 16th, 2000, I fatally shot and killed lil' Will while defending myself from a volley of gunfire and robbery attempts. After a little over two years of being in college I was now on the lam and once again looking at the death penalty if captured.

On the Lam

J uly 16th, 2000, I would awake this morning oblivious to the tragedy that would occur by the day's end. Little did I realize that by 7 p.m. that evening I would again be wanted for murder and on the lam for the next three months. Eventually, I would turn myself in to face persecution and wrongful conviction in connection with what the media would describe as a drive-by slaying which resulted in the death of William B. Anderson.

William Bentley Anderson Jr, a.k.a. lil' Will, was a 20 year old kid from Oakland who, like myself when his age, hung out with the wrong crowd. I had met him the summer of 2000 as a result of my job as a maintenance man and on-site manager for a small apartment complex in West Oakland. His parents, seemingly good Christian folks, had rented an apartment in the building. At the time the owner of the apartment complex and I did not realize they had actually rented it for Will and his Uncle Bill. Eventually, when this was discovered, the owner opted to evict them.

By now I had grown fond of the Anderson family. Will's father, a prominent minister, was a proud man reserved yet cordial and easy to speak with. His mother, Mrs. Anderson, was a woman of vision and hope who struck me to be the driving force behind both Junior and Senior's ambition. I recall vividly the day they were moving out of the apartment complex. Mrs. Anderson and I were making small talk as I attempted to navigate the awkwardness of having to evict a family I had grown fond of.

Prior to this, there were many days that Bill and I would sit on the steps of the apartment complex and smoke a blunt and drink a beer. We would make small talk about life, politics, and his concern for his nephew, who he believed you would eventually "get killed". Just hearing him say that would always make me cringe inside because we both knew what lil' Will was doing in the streets. I had come to know enough about the young Anderson's activities to know that he and I were like mixing oil with water and that I needed to distance myself from him for his own sake.

Will, despite being the son of a prominent minister, was an amateur Jack artist who often boasted about the robberies he and his crew pulled off. "I put that pistol right upside their head and make them strip," he would always boast. Me, I was selling a few pounds of marijuana here-and-there and in an effort to work my way out of the game, I was attending college and opening my first clothing boutique.

That day as the Anderson family were moving out, Mrs. Anderson and I were talking about my plans. She had seen me at work renovating the storefront that sat under the apartment building. After explaining to her my plans, she would compliment my efforts stating, "You know… That's good baby. William needs to be doing what you are doing instead of running the streets." It made me proud to hear someone acknowledging my efforts considering all I had gone through to get there. At the same time there was a part of me that feared what would ever happen if lil' Will ever trained his sights on me as a potential mark. His Uncle Bill and I had often spoke about how his activities were going to get him killed. Deep down inside I had a gut feeling, a feeling that would later come back to haunt me, that I could very well wind up killing him because he mistook me for something I was not—a victim!

***

Sunday, July 9th, 2000. A week prior to the shooting. I walk into the apartment building after returning from the corner store. Will and one of his cohorts are coming down the stairs at a quick pace leading into the lobby. Seeing one another, he would greet me with surprise and claim he is there to pick up his family's mail. I had been collecting it since they were evicted and had been storing it in an office space in the building that was being renovated. No sooner I pulled the keys out of my pocket and unlocked the door, Will's partner hauls off and strikes me in the side of the head with a stiff right punch. Instantly, I stumbled forward and the struggle ensued between the three of us.

We would tussle for what seemed like an eternity before Will eventually managed to pull a pistol out and demand I "strip". Realizing I had got caught slipping and was on the unfortunate end of a gun barrel, I immediately complied and handed over my wallet. Like that, just as quickly as it started, it was over and I would watch them turn and disappear out the building. As if what had just happened was not enough to shatter my sense of security, what I was to learn next would put me on the edge even more.

After being assaulted and robbed, I eventually pulled myself together and slowly climbed the stairs leading to my apartment. I recall vividly as if yesterday how I struggled with the lock before my sister eventually swung open the door and cried aloud in relief before explaining to me that Will had just attempted to force his way into the apartment. After settling her down she went on to explain how had it not been for the door chain and her fighting him off, he would have easily got in.

Oakland being a city where murder-robbery is commonplace, up until that point I had considered myself fortunate to have walked away from the skirmish with just a few bruises and a swollen jaw. Yet after learning what had just happened with my sister, I needed to regain my sense of security. So I did what any sensible human being would have done—I immediately purchased a gun.

Additional security protocols would be implemented. Later that day I would build a sturdy barricade on the door and request of the owner to change the lock on the security gate because I suspected Will had gained entry into the building with an extra copy key. I also began making plans to move into another apartment at one of the owner's other buildings.

Over the next few days my behavior could best be described as somewhat skittish and paranoid. Both my family and I were living in constant fear of being attacked. My fiancée and I slept with a gun over the bed rest. When leaving the apartment building, day or night, we would have friends guard us with it or I would carry it myself to and fro. Indeed, I was very cautious in my travels. Even around the neighborhood I would not walk to the local store by myself or allow my sister or fiancée to do so. Even more, I made sure that they all knew how to use the gun.

Friday, July 14th, 2000. I was again attacked. Thi assault and robbery attempt would occur outside the apartment building. That day I had been explaining to some friends what was going on when I received a phone call that someone wanted to take a look at one of the cars that I was selling. They claimed that they were waiting outside and asked if I could step out. Once outside, I checked my mailbox at the back of the building and that's when I was ambushed. Will and two of his cohorts, one of which was Terry Dandy, demanded money. Instantly the struggle broke out. As we struggled, Terry would pull out a pistol and strike me with the butt in the left eye. Instantly I cried out. That's when my company upstairs looked out the second story window and I yelled up for them to throw me my gun. Will, Terry and the other guy instantly took off running before a small group of neighbors quickly gathered to figure out what all the commotion was about. Eventually, things would settle down and I would make my way back upstairs to tend to my wounds. I was now in an even more intense state of shock and dismay at William's brazen attacks and realized I desperately needed to do something before my family or I came up seriously injured or worse, dead.

Sunday, July 16th, 2000. I woke that morning around 7 a.m. to take my fiancée to work. As usual, I took the gun with us. The drive over to the bank where she worked was uneventful. I returned all the same and immediately went to work on my storefront, cleaning and painting. Time quickly flew by and before long I would be joined by a couple of my associates and my sister. Whereas, we worked off and on throughout the day.

Later that afternoon I got a call from my fiancée to pick her up from work. She had decided to take off early to help out with the store. Despite everything that was going on, we were all pretty excited about opening day, which was a month out. Somehow, I had managed to push all the drama with Will to the back of my mind and enjoy the rest of the day. Dinnertime soon approached so my fiancée decided to order pizza for everyone while my associates and I decided to make a last-minute run to Home Depot to buy some supplies.

Off we went to Emeryville. After completing our shopping I asked one of my associates to pull the car around to the loading dock so we could get the supplies loaded while I paid for them. After everything was loaded, I jumped in the back seat of the car and we headed home. That's when everything went left.

As we approached 30th and San Pablo Boulevard, one of my associates noticed Will and a few of his partners standing by the phone booth. Before we knew what was happening all hell breaks loose and shots rang out. Terry, who was standing on the corner next to Will, had started shooting on sight. Without even thinking, I snatched up the shotgun and returned fire, fatally striking Will as Terry turned in response to my gunfire and disappeared into traffic.

***

Atlanta, Georgia. It was a long and tumultuous ride. For four days I rode a Greyhound bus, heart racing and nerves shot. The Oakland Police Department and the federal authorities were in hot pursuit. My fiancée, whose family were Mexican and Nicaraguan immigrants, had been visited by the OPD and FBI. They informed the U.S./Mexico border agencies had been notified and wanted posters had been placed at every major checkpoint.

Looking back, I recall jumping on a bus in San Francisco and landing in Los Angeles hours later after having shot and killed Will. It was brutal! Undercover agents stood out like sore thumbs. When they swooped in, my heart skipped a beat. Just like that I thought it was all over. Yet the Game God had my back. Standing in line just a few feet ahead of me was a young trap star, who I would later learn was from Birmingham, Alabama. He had traveled to California to pick up 30 pounds of Los

Angeles dirt weed. To his genius, he had mailed it back home. The DEA would come up short this day and I would continue with my travels.

Next would be Flagstaff, Arizona, Dallas, Shreveport, and Memphis, Tennessee—all hotspots for Greyhound bus station drug bust. Unscathed, I slid through: packed, compressed and sealed with several pounds of marijuana and a thousand ecstasy pills concealed in the lining of my duffel bag. Eventually, I would touch down in Atlanta and quickly learn I was in the middle of a major trap spot.

Across the street from the bus station, stood Magic City—notorious strip club. Lamborghinis, Mercedes-Benzes, and an assortment of luxury vehicles lined the Peachtree thoroughfare. Behind the station was the MARTA train, which touched all major points of DeKalb County. Within an hour of arriving, I would connect with family and for the next few weeks I would tour the city's trap spots. I would walk into a den of wolves, throw down my product, collect and bounce to the next state, Florida. With the threat of arrest looming over my head, I was forced to push the fear of the unknown to the back of my mind.

In just three months I had undergone yet another transformative life experience. Ironically, both tragedy and growth would come of it. The tragedy, William Bentley Anderson had lost his life to the streets of West Oakland. There, we both had accepted a way of life that neither he nor I truly understood. Neither of us were conscious of the cultural forces that guided our worldview. Neither of us understood how they controlled and predicted our behavior outcomes. And neither of us would escape the consequences they created for us to be beholden to.

As for how this experience impacted me growth wise? It is no secret that fear can push one into many dangerous situations when you are on the run. The paranoia, the uncertainty, the need to survive alone will drive you over the top. Fear often controls. It hinders personal growth. For most of my life fear had always been a driving force compelling me to step outside my comfort zone. Essentially, I allowed this and other circumstances to control me. I became a reaction. After being on the lam and allowing fear to force me into some rather dangerous situations, I realized that in order to have courage, one must possess fear. It was then that I began to place in context the fact that I had to stop allowing it to control me. Instead, I had to develop the courage to control it and the circumstances it lead me to. For the first time in my life I began to realize I could be in control of circumstances instead of them in control of me.

Training Ground

November 2000, I'm again arrested for first-degree murder. After almost two years of college in the Bay Area, a sense of defeat has swept over me in light of my current situation: I'm now a number in the nation's third-largest county jail, Santa Rita. For the next four years, it would become a university of radical thought and study. Here, I would quickly learn the dangers of studying in a sterile college environment—the distinction between learning in a college classroom opposed to a prison after having been afforded the luxury of time and a well-stocked Alameda County Public Library program offered at the jail. Consequently, the 26 year old kid would become immersed in the tomes of Black Panther history, Steve Biko, Nelson Mandela, Che Guevara and Fidel Castro, and many other political disciplines, including the very prisoners I was incarcerated with. And so the story goes....

Don't judge the messenger, judge the message... the adage aptly applied to my experience in the county lockup. Had it not been for my ability to do so, I would have missed out on the plethora of oral history I would be exposed to by the brothers who filled the jail. Sadly, many had succumbed to addiction of some sort. King Heron had devastated. It seemed as if eight out of ten of my cell mates were tore up off that dog food. They were the children of former Black Panther Party members and knew all too well the history.

Often they would share with me their stories of eating breakfast at the Black Panther Party Breakfast Program or how they attended the Black Panther schools or other community programs. For them these stories were ceremonial to share with me or any other poor sap in the pod that would listen. For the youngsters, they were simply dope fiends living off the hype of an era that played a role in shaping the "City of Dope". For me personally, it was an opportunity to get some understanding as to what the pivotal point, that is the point where one of the most revolutionary movements in American history had retrogressed into a story of murder, corruption and implosion.

Amongst my jail mates there were the many who were well-versed in the history and forces that would decimate the Party. They knew what books I needed read and study to satisfy my curiosity. Even more, they would engage me in debate and often a suggestion: *Seize the Time* by Bobby Seale, *Soul On Ice* by Eldridge Cleaver, *Revolutionary Suicide* by Huey P Newton, *Taste of Power* by Elaine Brown, and many many others including the disciplines and historiographies of the Cuban Revolution, Steve Biko's discourses on Black Power vs Black Consciousness, Karl Marx's Manifesto and more.

Assisting the process was the Alameda County Public Library. Oh how I took delight in the book program it offered at the jail. Once a month the librarians would visit and bring hundreds books to dispense to the population. I recall how there always seemed to be a title or two I would find on the cart that would open my mind to the vistas of thought I had never even imagined. I was simply astonished with all the different genres of books they would bring in. There would be books on marketing and financing, Political Science and history, world leaders, and then too there was the cowboy and urban literature: Donald Goines, Longarm and of course the local writers.

Best of all was the fact that if you were looking for a particular title, and it was not on the cart, you could submit a request and it would be delivered the following month. And if it was not in stock they would buy it for you brand new. Man, talking about a kid in a candy store. Reading became my escape from not only the situation I was in but so too the traps of my ignorance that I had allowed to condemn me once again. Realizing this, I would read for days on the end; sometimes for 24 hours straight!

During this time, while there was not one person that had a significant influence on me, there was the typical character. My jail mates and I were men of consequence: poverty, the War on Drugs, and Cointelpro.[1] Usually, they would come in off the streets hardened by these circumstances and, within a day or two, the withdrawal symptoms would surface. Fortunately, I kept a "get back kit" composed of fruit, candy and hygiene to assist with their recovery.

---

[1] **COINTELPRO** (syllabic abbreviation derived from COunter INTELligence PROgram) (1956–1979, and beyond) is a series of covert and illegal[1][2] projects conducted by the United States Federal Bureau of Investigation (FBI) aimed at surveilling, infiltrating, discrediting, and disrupting American political organizations.[3][4] FBI records show COINTELPRO resources targeted groups and individuals the FBI deemed subversive,[5] including feminist organizations,[6] the Communist Party USA,[7] anti–Vietnam War organizers, activists of the civil rights movement or Black Power movement (e.g. Martin Luther King Jr., the Nation of Islam, and the Black Panther Party), environmentalist and animal rights organizations, the American Indian Movement (AIM), independence movements (such as Puerto Rican independence groups like the Young Lords), and a variety of organizations that were part of the broader New Left and unrelated groups such as the Ku Klux Klan.[8]

Once they got a few hot meals in them, did a few push-ups and got their numbers up with whatever click they belong to, the old revolutionary con artist would resurface. Then too, there was the dope fiend jack-artist, with a drug-free conscious, who became the self-appointed pod leader. For them, "priority" was dictating who got to use the comrades' phone, read the newspaper first or determine what channel the TV would stay on. As to be expected, there were many intense standoffs and fights.

One day I was standing in a small circle of onlookers observing a domino game. Having observed my astute character and ability to hold my own, one of these revolutionary con artists approached me and asked, "Why haven't you come home, folks?" It was a Bay Area phrase used by gang members to recruit. My response? "What I look like being a sucker for another nigga's cause!" Instantly all he'll broke loose before my cellie, who was part of this dude's click, stepped in an restored the peace after checking his comrade for getting at me like that.

All in all, it would be four years of intense study in the Alameda County Jail. There, and in spite of the con game ran by the many self-appointed pod leaders and diplomats, I would gain tremendous insight into the school of radical thought. It would be the second stage in the development of my political consciousness; the first being my previous gang ties in Oklahoma. Thereafter, the lense on my view of the world would shift. I begin to understand more and more the nature of the political forces that had been holding me captive both physically and mentally. What would come next could only be described as my enlistment into an extremely radical political climate—the California prison system.

San Quentin & New Folsom State Prison

After 20 years of incarceration, I have observed how these two prisons serve distinct political purposes for the California Department of Corrections & [r]ehabilitation. Whereas, San Quentin over the years has transitioned from one of the most violent prisons in America to that of a model prison.

In contrast, New Folsom, a maximum security prison, stands at the epicenter of the department's intent to stir controversies to justify measures and expenditures to control violent criminals. Naturally, the dynamic in these two prisons is as different as day and night despite the fact they both house supposedly dangerous people. So what contributes to the violent atmosphere of one opposed to the relatively tranquil environment of the other? This question, I can only hope to answer with my prison experience having served time in them both and how it facilitated my understanding of their impact and the dehabilitating effect on countless individuals, including myself.

***

2006, I'm sitting in a prison cell at New Folsom, a.k.a. California State Prison Sacramento, which is located in Folsom, California. It is one of the most notorious prisons in the state, if not the nation, with a long history of violence housing some of California's most dangerous prisoners. Built in 1986, New Folsom is a maximum and super-maximum security prison. A significant number of the state's Security Housing Unit (SHU) kick out prisoners often land here in one of its 180-design yards.

To better understand, a 180-design is a highly isolated and controlled housing unit. Whereas, a unit is divided into three, 40 Man, two per cell, cubicles with a in-house guard tower stationed with a Mini-14 assault rifle and two floor officers equipped with an assortment of non-lethal flash grenades, tear gas, stab-proof vests and riot gear.

There is a two-tier security classification that prisoners in a 180-design are assigned to: One, the SHU, a supermax tantamount to solitary confinement, whereas we are confined to a cell 163 of 168 hours that make up a week. Generally, we are allowed three days of outside cell activity. There are no contact visits and restricted movement (I.e., shackled) to-and-from the yard, library, and medical clinic. You are shackled from head to toe every step of the way. The second security classification is the above-mentioned which is a mid-level supermax. The difference between the 180-design in the SHU is minimal. The 180 permits unrestricted, that is without chains, yet controlled movement to access contact visits, the yard, law library, phone calls, etc. during designated times throughout the day;

allowing outside cell activity. Then too, there are inmate job assignments and some self-help activities. For example, Alcoholic Anonymous and Narcotics Anonymous, which allow us to remain outside of the cell during evening hours. Typically, on a 180-design, we would get two hours of yard program every other day, which was infrequent and subject to lockdowns due to repeated instances of violence.

August 2004, I arrived at New Folsom after a two-hour bus ride on the Grey Goose from San Quentin's Reception Center. Within a few months of arriving, I would witness a prisoner shot dead by a guard. Thereafter, the next few months would be spent trying to get a grip on my surroundings. I had learned from my stay in Santa Rita that the California prison system was highly political and a place where both guards and prisoners alike vie for turf. Racial lines were drawn: Blood Alley, Crip area, Bay Area area, non-affiliate area, Wood Pile (as in "Peckerwood"), and the South Side Mexican area. No one, absolutely no one crossed the lines. Rarely, did a guard even cross the yard into these areas. And it was for good reason.

These areas were not simply designated for social reasons. No! They were mainly designated, that is segregated, for "removals". A removal meant violence. If you were in bad standing, snitched or owed a drug debt, for example, the odds were you would get the shit beat out of you or worse, you would get stabbed! Within the first year at New Folsom I would witness countless removals. The knife play was vicious. On average there would be two to three removals a week. Blood stained the entire yard. Warning shots were often fired. Non-lethal rubber bullets whizzed across the yard daily and struck indiscriminately. Shit got real quick!

One of the first and most important lessons I was to learn to survive this madness came via another prisoner who was a member of the Black Guerilla Family. He had over 20 calendars under his belt. I recall vividly as he stood outside my cell door and we made introductions the day I arrived. Within a week, he had grown comfortable enough with me to approach me and pull my coat tail. "Ivan," he said, "bro you ain't from California! Keep it that way! Don't get involved in politics! Don't click up with none of these gangs!

Because it's all a bunch of problems and bullshit!" He went on to explain what, in time, I would learn about the "poli-tricks" and treachery had within each click. Years later it would be summed up by one of my cellies, "I love you today, fuck you tomorrow!" It was a cutthroat environment no doubt. And it was not just the prisoners that were poli-tricking.

2015, "...the violence is coming back!" This was talk amongst the staff who were complaining about a recent federal court decision in the Asker v. Brown that had deemed indefinite solitary confinement unconstitutional. Prison officials were now being forced to release some 1,500 prisoners from the SHU.

At the time I did not really understand what all the fuss was about. Then one day a blood gang member I had known for years came to me and said, "Hey Ive... we need to speak to the captain about what's going on on this yard." He went on to observe how an influx of white supremacist gang members were being inserted into the yard at a disproportionate numbers.

In terms of numbers, how it worked on a 180 yard, typically you would have 30 Southside Mexicans,

30 hardline white boys and 60 blacks from different gangs and cliques per housing unit because the Southsiders and the whites clicked together. Therefore, if there was ever any conflict we would not be outnumbered. Yet the administration had another trick up their sleeve. This influx of hardline white supremacist eventually led to an imbalance in the numbers. So what happened next was me and blood went and addressed the issue with the captain. After issuing us assurances that the numbers would balance out, we went along our way.

A week later I was transferred off the yard. We were now being informed that the reason why they were moving blacks around was because they were getting ready to insert some high profile prisoners and would need extra security to monitor the situation for potential violence. Just so happened that high profile prisoner was none other than Hugo "Yogi" Pinell of the San Quentin Six.

The San Quentin Six were: Hugo "Yogi" Pinell, Willie Tate, Johnny Larry Spain, David Johnson, Fleeta Drumgo and Luis Talamantez, who were accused of participating in an August 21, 1971 *escape* attempt at San Quentin that left six people dead, including *George Jackson*, a co-founder of the *Black Guerrilla Family*. The ensuing trial would cost more than $2 million and has been noted as the longest trial in California history, lasting some 16-months *trial*. It was dubbed "The Longest Trial" by *Time Magazine*.

During the escape, which sparked a *riot* on the cellblock, Jackson was reported to have had a .32 caliber pistol smuggled into the prison by attorney *Stephen Bingham*. Immediately after the incident, Bingham went on the run and fled the country for 13 years; he returned in 1984 to stand trial, and was acquitted of all charges in 1986. Bingham's defense had argued that guards had smuggled Jackson the gun, hoping that he would be killed.

During the ensuing riot, Jackson, three corrections officers, and two inmates were killed. In addition to Jackson, those killed in the altercation were guards Paul E. Krasenes, 52, Frank DeLeon, 44, and Jere P. Graham, 39, as well as inmates John Lynn, 29, and Ronald L. Kane, 28. Spain was found guilty in the shooting deaths of guards DeLeon and Graham, Pinell was convicted of cutting the throats of guards Charles Breckenridge and Urbano Rubiaco, Jr. (died 2013), both of whom survived, and Johnson was convicted of assaulting Breckenridge. There were no convictions for the killings of Krasenes, Lynn, or Kane. Drumgo, Talamantez, and Tate were found not guilty of all charges, including various counts of murder, conspiracy, and assault.

A few weeks later I would be in the hole. It was August 21st the anniversary of George Jackson's murder at San Quentin. What was to transpire thereafter, when Yogi was inserted of the yard, would be an immediate lockdown, threats and an explosion of violence. Whereas, a full scale race riot would result in him being stabbed to death by white supremacist gang members. This was one of the coldest setups I ever seen in terms of the games that the administration play. They literally set him up to be murdered and I would soon learn myself just how treacherous the *Green Wall* was.

The Green Wall is a common term used to refer to California correctional officers who practice a "code of silence" and operate as a criminal gang within the prison system. Their tactics include, but are not limited to, setting prisoners up to be assaulted by other prisoners as was the case with Yogi who the administration inserted into a yard of white supremacist dead set on exacting revenge after he had allegedly assaulted a number of white supremacist during the seventies. These tactics also include revealing a prisoners paperwork and dropping kites on prisoners. The latter I was to learn as it was the reason I was in the hole.

THE GAMES PRISON STAFF PLAY:
CROSS ARTIST 101

I know many of you are wondering why you have not heard from me lately. Well, truth is I have been weathering the storm. Seems my book *Domestic Genocide: The Institutionalization of Society* has been making quite the stir amongst prison officials. On June 22nd, an anonymous kite was received by the administration claiming I was quote on quote, "coordinating and organizing the inmate population to attack staff and take back the institutions thru (sic) blood." Apparently, my book was mentioned as some sort of guerrilla guide to accomplish this. Wow! Now that's heavy. I could not have thought of a better promotional gimmick myself. Obviously, whoever wrote the kite had not read the book. Nonetheless, the controversy this created has worked to the advantage of not only promoting it, but has also brought awareness to the injustices prisoners of color suffer at the hands of racist prison administrators. Peep how they twist your boy!

Consequently, I have been thrown in the hole indefinitely pending an investigation this so-called anonymous kite. Despite the serious nature of the matter, I had to laugh in light of the fact it was reportedly typed up and made to appear as if it had been created on an inmate typewriter. Yeah, we still have those outdated machines in here. Thing is, seldom, if ever, do prison snitches type up kites. From what I *gather, they are generally handwritten. Again, I had to laugh because several officers and I quickly surmised this was the doing of staff in light of recent events which transpired over the course of the past few months.*

During which, prison officials have been on a persistent witch-hunt, searching my cell for contraband (I.e., a cell phone) and monitoring my various social media websites, blogs, radio interviews, and of course reviewing the book in hopes of finding something to confine me to a more restrictive housing unit. Undoubtedly, I have struck a chord with these Neo-Nazi correctional officers who aim to suppress my advocacy and support for the Black Lives Matter Movement. Ultimately, they came up with nothing. No promoting violence, no criminal or gang activity. Nothing!

Disappointed, the administration, particularly one Captain J. Stewart, then saw to issue a rules violation report for all things: authoring books that are for sale on the internet for profit. Now imagine that! Here it is that not only are the proceeds from my books donated to a charitable cause, but just a year ago, the California Department of Corrections and [r]ehabilitation received a $1 million dollar Grant from the William James Foundation to fund arts and creative writing classes at this prison.

So where did the plot to frame me and the kite come together? On June 12th, Stewart had me transferred to another facility knowing that, ultimately it would result in my placement in administrative segregation due to the fact that I had a documented security threat assessment on staff who worked there, which prohibited my warehousing on that yard. Within days of placement, and my repeated attempts to inform the administration of the situation, the kite gets dropped and I have been in the hole ever since. I have to admit it's been one hell of a roller coaster ride. And the worst is yet to come given my advocacy "can't stop, won't stop" nor be deterred by these events which in all actuality, have worked to my favor to create an opportunity to educate a number of prison staff, particularly white staff, who I consider to be decent human beings, on the impeding factors and genocidal nature of institutional racism.

—Ivan Kilgore, July 2015

After spending close to a decade housed in one of the nation's most violent prisons, I had learned the ropes of survival and gained the respect and trust of both prisoners and staff alike.

College In Prison

January 2018, Salinas Valley State Prison: The Fall season of the prison college program was set to begin. Despite having done an extensive self-study in the field of sociology, I had signed up for an introductory course. The plan was to access a potential resource given the limitations of my confinement. It was a long shot and I could only have hoped to have the fortune of building a bridge with a professor. Yet the day I walked into the classroom I instantly felt a tad bit optimistic and confident that I would be able to accomplish my goals when the professor introduced herself.

Before the class stood Megan McDrew. Tall, intelligent, and more importantly, a radical white girl with an inclination for prison abolition, I would later learn she was the daughter of a former CIA director. As I sat listening to her introduce herself, I looked around the classroom and realized few, if any, of my peers had the foggiest idea as to the ideological concepts, authors, and organizations that she was discussing. As she continued to discuss the course curriculum and class expectations, her mention of Angela Davis, Craig Haney, Mumia Abu-Jamal and a number of other players in the radical world of prison theory, was surreal. This woman was talking my language. I knew we would hit it off well. So I thought.

When I approached Megan after class that day and introduced myself as an author, founder and activist, she blew me off. See saw right through my bullshit. I was attempting to impress her. Not one to be defeated, I handed her a copy of my book *Domestic Genocide* and informed her of the prominent professors and activist I had worked with when writing it. She took the book, briefly looked it over, then handed it back to me with a few encouraging words. Damn!

Over the course of the next few weeks she and I would continue the charade. I met her at every twist and turn she threw at me: from the organizations, the events, the books, and people she mentioned, I made it a point to inform her that in many cases I either knew of them or personally knew the founders, sponsors, etc. When she lectured, I had to fight to keep my hand down. Eventually she relented and jokingly suggested I should be the one teaching the class. Of course, thereafter, I would become the teacher's pet.

By now I had decided to surprise her by sending a few copies of my book for her to read and pass out to the faculty at the University of California, Santa Cruz where she also taught. My game plan was hopefully the book would inspire her or other professors to possibly arrange several lectures with me. I will never forget her walking into the classroom flabbergasted the week after she received them. Almost immediately, she came over to me and said, "I can't believe you actually wrote this book. It's amazing! Have you ever considered doing any lecture presentations?" At that moment a sense of accomplishment swept over me as I recognized within myself an ability to manifest opportunity. I had stayed the course, thinking with my big head instead of the little one, which for my peers had proven difficult.

Watching Megan walk into the prison each week, beautiful and daring, was somewhat of a spectacle to observe. Each day she stood before the class kindly declining the advances of men who, like myself, had been deprived of a woman's grace and presence for years, if not decades. We all marveled at her beautifully shaped long legs and gossiped like women. For me these conversations were often a platform to address how prison had stunted our maturity when it came to interacting with the opposite sex. Indeed, I had to keep it respectful and maintain my focus. But it, by no measure, was easy.

Part of what kept me focused was realizing just how much of an opportunity she and I could create for both prisoners and students. Plus, I had a vision for my organization; and that vision was I aimed to start an internship program with the University of California, Santa Cruz. Then too, part of what kept me focused was the fact that I had had a previous situation where, some 12 years prior, I had blew such an opportunity with *San Francisco Chronicle* reporter Meredith May by thinking with my little head. Still and yet, I entertained the locker room talk with the fellas as they plotted and schemed to woo her. It was comical and yet reassuring to know there was no true competition in a real sense knowing that they did not understand where her interests lie.

I remember one prisoner in particular just swore up and down that he had what it took to win her over. So every week, there we where sitting in class watching as he would skin-and-grin in her face and attempt to woo her with poems and pictures of himself dressed to the nines as a street hustler. It was comical. When that failed occasionally he would share with me his schemes and poetry. He was a very talented poet. Very talented. But unfortunately he just did not recognize where her interests lie. So I had to spell it out to him one day:

Bro... You realize prison has stunted our growth... See a lot of that flash and drag we used on the streets as youngn's to attract those bops and hoes, ain't flying with her. She's an educated woman committed to the struggle. More importantly, she is married. She got character man... Recognize that! Recognize her interests and understand why she and I have a platonic attraction. I got a real game plan here. I'm creating an opportunity with this woman, that she clearly recognizes the mutual benefit in as well as the effort I have put into it. It is because of this and the fact that we are like-minded in many ways that she is game for the play....

Of course, I also had to explain to him the mistake I had made with Meredith and how because of that experience it allowed for me to gain a certain level of maturity and professionalism that prison typically did not offer when it came to refraining from the egotistical pursuit of women.

All in all things would eventually pan out. Shortly after completing the course, Megan would arrange for me to present to her sociology students at Santa Cruz. Eager, I was more than prepared! In the years prior I had taken *Toastmasters*, an internationally renowned public speaking course. Whereas, during the fall and summer of 2014 I was able to test the waters with my verbals.

As it so happened, every year there would be a number of visiting groups of 40 or so criminal justice students who would tour the prison. There, at New Folsom, I would eventually find myself creating yet another opportunity to hone in on my skills and abilities to speak publicly. And yet, these presentations would result from a tumultuous relationship I had developed with a guard, Ricky Mendoza.

Mendoza, "a.k.a. Pretty Ricky," was a 30-year veteran. September 2011, I will never forget. He was working overtime in our housing unit on B-facility at New Folsom. I had been housed in the facility for a little over six years at the time and it was my training ground: a 101 in radical literature, developing political consciousness, weapons manufacturing, gang and psychological warfare, combat training, and inside/outside structure development—that is, organizing human resources both inside and outside of prison walls.

That day, as Mendoza made his rounds, a nurse and he walked past my cell only to be thrown into a state of utter shock and confusion. Instantly, the nurse screamed at the top of her lungs in fear after looking into my cell. Inside, my cellie and I are locked up like pit bulls in a vicious dog fight. Only I had a knife and was intent on killing the motherfucker. Mendoza quickly radioed for backup, "inmate being assaulted with a weapon." When it was all said and done with my tough-guy cellie was not as tough as he thought. He had 13 puncture wounds from an eight-inch shank, a punctured lung and a pumpkin head and got 11 day hospital stay with a tube in his chest for thinking I was a pussy. A head full dreadlocks drenched with two canisters of pepper spray and a 12 month SHU would be my final disposition.

Eight months later, I was released from the SHU back to B-facility. Upon seeing Mendoza, there was a newfound appreciation for one another. Within weeks, he gave me a volunteer clerk's detail in the gym and allowed me to use an old computer station for a hour a week to format the manuscript to complete *Domestic Genocide*. With no TV, radio or distractions, I had been able to complete the book while I was in solitary confinement. Occasionally, he would read a few pages then comment or make suggestions as I pecked away on that old computer.

Almost a year later, I will never forget how his face lit up with a sense of accomplishment when I reported to work one morning with the finished product in hand polished and published. Seeing my dedication and knowing that I was low-key, Mendoza would eventually introduce me to a visiting group of college students from the University of California, San Diego Criminal Justice Department. They were part of Professor Paul Sutton's *Prison Tours Program* which had been operating throughout the California Prison system for some thirty years.

By the time I presented to Mcgan's sociology class, I was more than prepared. I was on the fast track to becoming a radical prisoner and these sessions and lecture presentations would become part of my training.

Becoming

Serving 20 years in prison on a wrongful conviction will definitely motivate you to fight injustice. Of course, this isn't always the case for every prisoner. What it took for me to make this transformation from drug dealer to advocate was a complex process of events and tragedy and prison. Though, I do not want to leave the reader with the impression that "prison" saved me or in some sense made me a better person. After spending two decades trapped within prison walls and experiencing all the dehumanization I often ask: Why is it people think that prison is a place where you learn to make good choices, pick good friends, be polite and respectful all the time?

Comrade Alan's Response:

Prison isn't where you learn to make 'good decisions.' It is a place you wind up warehoused as you await the day you will ultimately die or be released. The only reason some (few) folks can make it through is due to sheer resilience born of their own accord, coping mechanisms they learned prior to coming in or during previous stays with others with their own coping mechanisms, and the love and support of others both inside and outside.

Prison taught me to hate disciplinarians. It taught me to challenge those who would arbitrarily fuck with me. Prison taught me to mute my true self to put on a front for the prison administrators, the guards, and my fellow incarcerated people.

I didn't learn manners, how to model better behaviors, or become a better more productive person simply because you locked me in a box. If I had the same reprieves and resources provided to me in healthier freer environments imagine just how much further I could've came. I became knowledgeable on making better choices, building more mutually beneficial relationships, and being polite and respectful DESPITE the violent environments I've been placed in.

I give no thanks to the prison industrial complex for who I am today. I give praise to those who stuck with me, who nourished me intellectually, emotionally, and spiritually while I was trapped in a cell. I know it was not the circumstances I was thrust into that made me who I am but the people who cared enough to show me a better way and who had the patience to support me through my struggles.

Prisons, courts, police departments --these are all houses of violence and they do nothing but foist the social mores and norms of a twisted colonialist society upon us. If the appearance of being obedient is what is deemed "respectful" and "polite", then I want no part of said politeness and respect. Attempting to beat people into submission and coerce them through abuse and trauma begets the same harm. I am who I am in spite of the attempts to force change in me by this carceral system.

Giving thanks to the prison system, to me as a formerly incarcerated person, feels like some form Stockholm syndrome. No thanks necessary for the oppressor. Praise for prisons causing positive change only emboldens and further entrenches the notion that the prison system is needed and the treatment we receive is deserved when we give it.

So what inspired me to start a nonprofit organization from prison? My response? A reputed leader of the notorious Chicago gang named Larry Hoover, the founder of the Gangster Disciples. I studied what he accomplished with the Gangster Disciples from a prison cell. Namely, a multi-state organization that federal authorities credited for some $100,000,000 annually in receipts built on a corporate structure. After reading his story, I came away with the notion that if he could do it, so could I. Only I would do it legitimately.

Thereafter, I will never forget I was sitting in my cell one day and my cellie, Shorty, who was from Los Angeles, asks me why I was writing a book? It was my first book project, *Domestic Genocide.* I explained to him that the book was simply a blueprint, that is, a doorway to a bigger plan which was to start an organization. "You cannot do that," he responded. At that moment my mind was made up. His comment was the fuel to the fire that was burning inside of me.

Of course I was a bit naïve as to all that would have to go into creating such an endeavor. In fact, I had the slightest clue. But then, as the adage goes: Where there is a will, there is a way. And so it began that day. From that day forth my time and energy would be spentidentifying what knowledge, skill set and resources I needed to accomplish my goal. Shortly, thereafter, Shorty would move out and I would get another cellie, a young kid from Inglewood California who was a blessing in disguise.

Santos was a talented artist. He could sing like The O'Jays. Draw like Picasso and had a fairly good head for business. From the day he walked into the cell, we instantly clicked and went to work. One day, he walks in from his job assignment with a 700 plus page book on how to start a nonprofit organization. "Man...where you get this?" I asked with surprise and eager. It was as if God was laying out the pieces to the puzzle before me. As could be expected, I would spend the next several months consuming that book as if it were a lifeline.

Soon, I was able to identify other areas that I needed to work on. One of which was becoming a skilled orator. If you were to ask anyone who knew me growing up they would tell you that I was a shy kid. Yet being in prison all these years had been forcing me out of my shell. I had become a skilled practitioner of law. I was becoming a skilled writer and now it was time for me to become a skilled orator.

One day I walk into the church hoping to find a venue to hone in on my skill. I grew up in a church and I had three uncles who were preachers. So the chapel was the first place I figured I would go in hopes of finding a place where I could become a better public speaker. For about a week or so I sat in the back pew awaiting the opportunity to present itself for me to take to the pulpit and give a sermon. It was common practice that the Chaplin would allow inmates to sometime do this. But that just was not going to happen for me. This was for a number of reasons. For one, I no longer had the interest of becoming a preacher even though I knew the Bible like the back of my hand. It just did not set right with me to use the pulpit to deliver my message. I wanted to be an activist.

Eventually, God would work wonders. The chaplain comes up to me one day, pulls me to the side and asks, "Would you be interested in a self-help group I'm going to start soon? It's a public speaking group." As it would turn out, the whole time he was planning to start a Toastmasters Gavel Club, which was an internationally known public speaking course. And so the story goes... over the course of the next six years I would go from being a participant to being a facilitator of the Gavel Club.

During this time, I would learn more than simply public speaking. Today I often tell people that Toastmasters had a series of exercises compiled in some ten or more manuals. Each manual dealt with various areas of leadership development and public speaking. There were manuals that dealt with how to craft the art of speaking on the radio or television. Then there were manuals on how to facilitate meetings; how to conduct a debate and so on and so forth. Then of course, there were many lessons gained from our sponsor, Chaplin Stewart.

Chaplin Stewart was a fairly decent man. African-American, dark-skinned and no more than 5'6" tall, he was as round as a black Santa Claus. Always one to cite scripture, he would always encouraged me to return to my roots. He was also a great mentor. Often, he would pull me to the side and provide me some insight or advice. "Always allow people to make a positive contribution. Even if it's not necessarily something that's needed," I vividly recall him advising me one day.

By the time I was finished with *Domestic Genocide*, I was more than ready to test the waters. After practicing on my cellies, the yard and staff, I looked on a crowd of criminal justice students as they walked out across the yard one day. This is where Pretty Ricky aka Officer Ricky Mendoza opened a door for me to begin my development and growth with working with universities. From that day forth each time a college group would appear at the prison I would be summoned to come in and give a speech about my life. Eventually, I would invite other members of our Toastmasters group to come in and speak as well. These opportunities gave us all the ability to gauge whether or not our speeches were being effective on audience and engaging. As time went on I would eventually go from being a shy kid to someone who could actually hold the floor and move a crowd.

***

When I finally made up my mind to write a book, I was fortunate to be able to fall back on the resourcefulness

I had learned from my grandparents. Immediately, begun the process of identifying what would be needed to start. Here is where I found myself in a creative writing class offered at the prison. Thereafter, there would be many days I would sit in a cramped little room, the size of a walk in closet, which was in the breezeway on C-yard at New Folsom. For six years we would convene to develop our writings. I recall the first piece I wrote and read in class. It was a piece from *Domestic Genocide* about my up bringing in Oklahoma. With each word that spilled from my pen, my pain, my story began to come together. Eventually, I would be a hundred, two-hundred, three-hundred pages into a manuscript. Before I realized it, it was time to get a typewriter.

Unfortunately, being in prison forces one to use such antiquated technology. Being the hustler I am, I remember my then cellmate coming into the cell one day with an old typewriter. "Say folks what you going to do with that?" I asked, knowing he had taken an interest in my CD collection. I then made a proposition he could not refuse. "Pick 5 CDs!" In all, it would cost me seven. Years later, after publishing the book, I would run across him again at another institution. Seeing the smile on his face when I showed him what I did with that typewriter was rewarding to us both.

Of course, along the way to publishing there were many other obstacles my incarceration presented. I recall another of my cellmates who inspired me to write. He was doing a 15-to-life bid for second-degree murder after fatally stabbing his daughter's mother to death. Everyday he would sit on the edge of his bunk and turn out pages of neatly handwritten chapters of a manuscript. Just being in the presence of his determination would ever encourage me to do the same. Eventually, we went our separate ways and about two years later he pulled up on me on another yard with some very important information that would forever change the direction of my life. It was a lulu.com print-out on how to self-publish.

The print-out spelled out every aspect, from formatting to what a JPEG file was to the process of setting up the manuscript for self-publishing a book. Fortunately, I had enough experience with computers before prison to understand the language. That, of course, presented the next hurdle. I did not have computer access and I was soon to discover that to get my manuscript professionally typed up and formatted and edited would cost an arm and a leg. So once again I had to get creative.

Just so happened there was a computer course on Microsoft Word and Excel being taught at the prison. Thereafter, I was able to take what skills I had learned while attending college and apply them to this endeavor to become a published author. Even more, I would discover a keen ability to tap into that resourcefulness I had developed over the span of my life which now allowed for me to cultivate my calling as an author, advocate and philanthropist.

Joining the Movement

Two weeks after George Jackson was fatally shot at San Quentin, on September 9th, 1971, the Attica Correctional Facility in upstate New York would explode in a fury of violence and rioting. Members of the Black Panthers, Young Lords, Black Muslims, and white radical prisoners had formed an alliance and seized control of the facility. Over the course of the next four days, more than forty people would be killed by the state police in an effort to retake the prison.

Thereafter, for the next 40 years, an aggressive policy of indefinite solitary confinement would sweep across the nation's prison system to silence the voice and activities of those prisoners who fought for racial equality and justice behind prison walls. According to Bonnie Kerness, director of the American Friends Service Committee's Prison Watch Project:

In 1975, after the tumultuous years of the Civil Rights Movement, the Vietnam War, and the prisoners' rights movement, Trenton State Prison (now New Jersey State Prison) established an administrative isolation unit for politically dissident prisoners. The warden and his staff decided to use this technique, which was modeled after a unit in Soledad Prison in California. The Management Control Unit housed those prisoners who had not broken institutional rules, but who were, as a result of their political convictions and expressions, seen to be a threat by prisoner administrators....[i]

For many, the Attica rebellion and death of George Jackson was considered to have marked the beginning of the end of prisoner led social movements. However, in 2011 and 2014 the California Prisoner Strikes would prove otherwise as some 30,000 prisoners of all racial backgrounds united in protest of the unjust administrative process that Kerness and many others across the nation have written off and rallied against on behalf of the countless prisoners who had been placed in solitary confinement.

By 2015, the synergy surrounding the Hunger Strikes had garnered enough political clout to force the California Department of Corrections & [r]ehabilitation to enter into a settlement agreement in a landmark federal civil rights case, Ashker v. Brown, which effectively abolished indefinite solitary confinement. Since "virtually all of the over 1600 prisoners then languishing in indeterminate SHU[s] [have been] released back into general population."[ii]

Notably, there were two other crucial aspects that came of this progressive movement: (1) the Agreement to End Hostilities, which is a binding agreement between all California prisoners to end the decades-long conflict that fueled many gang wars; and (2) the energy and strengthening of the 'belief' that the prisoner-class—as a collective—has the power to abolish many of the oppressive and inhumane aspects of their incarceration. Moreover, the latter would eventually inspire the nation's prison population to engage in a series of resistance strategies to undermine the prison industrial complex.

On September 9th, 2016, the 45th anniversary of the Attica uprising, prisoners across the nation engaged in collective behavior–a series of protests against their captivity, exploitation, and the poor living conditions in many American prisons. According to David Fathi of the ACLU National Prison Project, it was the "largest prison strike in recent memory." [iii] BBC News Magazine, CNN and *The Guardian* estimated the number of inmates affected ranged from 20,000 to 50,000, to as high as 72,000, and affected an estimated 46 prisons in eleven states. [iv]

There were a number of anti-incarceration and prisoners' organizations such as Critical Resistance, the National Lawyer's Guild, the Industrial Workers of the World Labor Union, and many many others that endorsed and supported the protest. At the center of them, all was the Free Alabama Movement (FAM).

In 2013, Alabama prisoners Melvin Ray and Robert Earl Council (aka, Kinetic Justice) founded FAM and began organizing fellow prisoners throughout the Alabama Department of Corrections (ADOC) to launch a series of direct action campaigns. FAM's defined goals, beyond improving prison living conditions and [demanding adequate] medical care, include[d] reducing overcrowding through prisoner releases; ending unpaid prison slave labor; overhauling the Parole Board and establishing parole criteria; and abolishing the death penalty and sentences of life without parole.[v]

In January 2014, with the assistance of family and supporters, FAM members successfully staged the first of a series of non-violent protests and work strikes at three ADOC facilities. (ibid.) Shortly thereafter, Melvin, Robert Earl, and I, were introduced by a mutual friend who, after reading *Domestic Genocide* and having taken interest in partnering with our organization, suggested we join forces.

Within a matter of days, FAM and the UBFSF began forming a national strategy to promote our activism and gain support for our organizations' respective goals. Together, we took contraband cell phones and began hosting a national blog talk radio show from our prison cells (I was in New Folsom, at the time). Whereas, a number of prisoners, advocates and entertainers from across the nation would discuss issues of mass incarceration, police brutality, education reform, and the REAL about what's happening in American prisons.

Realizing the public would be distrustful of our allegations of rogue prison guards, etc., Melvin and Robert Earl filmed and recorded over 60 videos and interviews in the ADOC, which ranged from unconstitutional living conditions to the warden saying he didn't give a fuck about prisoner rights. Needless to say, this eventually set fire to the seats of Alabama Senator Cam Ward, Alabama Governor Robert Bently, the U.S. Department of Justice, and would cause the guards at several Alabama prisons to strike and refuse to report to work after the warden and several guards were stabbed in a riot at the William C. Holman Correctional Facility.[vi]

Since, the movement has gone viral! Here, I observed how the theory of technological determinism was instrumental in catapulting this prison movement onto the national and international stage. With the advantage of cell phone video technology and other technological advancements, such as social media, podcasting, and the print press, the once unsubstantiated/denied excessive force claim or, in the instant matter, the unconstitutional living conditions within the ADOC, were irrefutable and, thus, prompted national and international outrage.

As the movement grew and prisoners around the nation began protesting, conducting worker stoppages, etc., we were better able to organize these events with the assistance of the IWW who, at the urging of Black anarchist and former Lorenzo KomBoa Ervin, formed an Incarcerated Worker's Organizing Committee (IWOC), which quickly burgeoned into a national/international organization, to assist us to combat, among other things, penal slavery.

Learning of the foregoing allowed for me to both identify and place in context the four stages to which

Armand Mauss defined social movements are developed: (1) the "incipient" stage—that is, when the public takes notice of a situation and defines it as a problem; (2) when they began to organize—or, in Mauss's words, to "coalesce"; (3) if successful they (i.e., social movements) are incorporated into institutions— they become "bureaucratized"; and (4) they "decline".[vii]

***

For those of us that become incarcerated prison activists, the situation will motivate and impact us unlike non-incarcerated activists or those who have never experienced what it is like to survive the cage. In my humble opinion, the longer one is subjected to such an injustice, the more consumed and invigorated he or she will become in the struggle for freedom and ridding the world of oppressive institutions.

Consequently, the notion of maintaining "balance" goes out the door. A personal life becomes seemingly expendable in face of the fact that with each passing day that you are in the cage the fear of dying in prison and the loss of family and friends and the constant dehumanization and violence of the mind and body eats at you; making it almost impossible to focus on anything or anyone who is not in the fight with you or who does not have the capacity or resilience to withstand the pressure that inevitably comes with the territory.

Advocacy, activism and abolition have become my calling as I march throughout the California prison system and learn the essentials of what it takes for me to remain resilient and escape the reality of the cage and maintain my dignity. Advocating with FAM, engaged in numerous pro se state and federal civil litigation, fighting for educational programs, and healthcare, I have evolved into a respected legal scholar and activist within the California prison system.

Building a Legacy

One day I was standing on the tier in the housing unit at Cimarron City Correctional Facility when a Muslim brother named Mohammed approached me. We had known one another for quite some time so, after greeting each other and making small talk, he asked, "I see you're building your body well, but what about your mind?" By now I had been in prison for about ten months after spending two years in the Seminole County Jail. I had become what we call in prison a "yard ape". In just that short period of time, some ten months, I had gained over 50 lbs. of muscle on a 5'9" frame, weighing in at 197 lbs. and was bench pressing 315 lbs. I was a beast!

That was some 23 years ago and yet the conversation with Brother Mohammad still resonates with me to this day. After taking a moment to reflect, I responded by informing him of my plans to attend college after I was released. I will never forget the look on his face after telling him this. It was a look of disappointment. For there were plenty of brothers in prison making penitentiary promises to attend college. Disappointed with my response, he calmly leaned on the rail of the tier, looked out across the dayroom and stated, "You're in a university now! Why aren't you studying?" Stubborn, I took a position that college would suffice; that it would provide me with an edge to succeed in the real world.

Needless to say, that conversation with Brother Mohammed would forever be etched into my memory because it forced me to acknowledge the fact that I had neglected to spend my time in prison wisely developing my conscious. Simply put, I had failed to study that which he was attempting to expose me to which was readily available right there amongst those brothers who, like himself, had spent decades behind the walls and concertina wire studying and analyzing the world before us.

Still and yet, I would eventually discharge my sentence and set out on a journey in search of knowledge and wisdom. Unknowingly, it would be a journey that was to send me into Oakland's ghettos, college hallways, and, eventually, land me back at square one. Whereas, after being sentenced to life without the possibility of parole, I would be forced to attack my ignorance head-on.

Some two decades later, I am on the eve of my 47th birthday and to great pains, struggle with the fact that I have spent the majority of my adult years in prison. When I look back on my life—my humble beginnings, school days, trappin', murder trials, etc.— there is now a sense of urgency and consciousness that has compelled me to embrace a higher calling to be part of the solution instead of the problem. My motivation to do so I attribute to my roots which, when you rot in a prison cell for decades, at some point, if not often, will force you to think about your core values.

Naturally, all the above brought me to a point in life where I was compelled to reflect on my legacy—that is, what I wanted to be remembered for when the etchings set on my gravestone. I began to realize that my footprints were going to be washed away in the tide of life because I had not gave due consideration to how I was living it. In fact, I was not living at all. I existed and was struggling to survive. What prison did was gave me time to take inventory, a hard look, at the fact that I had become a statistic, a number with little value amongst my community and peers. It was then that I became determined to change not only my plight but those of others.

A magnificent discovery indeed, this in and of itself would instantly change my focus. No longer was I chiefly concerned with the material things in life. I realized that they were a carrot on a stick controlling and driving me down a path of destruction.

Often, I tell people about this moment, this time and space, when it finally "clicked" and the light shined on me. It was the summer of 2006. I was six years in on a life sentence. There I was lying on my bunk at New Folsom, Facility-B, Housing Unit 4, cell 101. Staring at the ceiling, I began thinking about where I was in life, how I had arrived there, and more importantly, what I was doing to change my predicament.

My cellie and I were what we call in prison "penitentiary rich". We had accumulated all those things that made for a comfortable living arrangement: 20 cases of Top Ramen soups, 50 to 75 pouches of meat products and other foodstuffs, a kitchen detail, 150 CDs, a boom box, a runner (I.e., a female who visited regularly and took care of our business on the outside), drugs, a knife, and of course, a cell phone. In terms of prison, we had it all figured out and were at the top of our game. So we thought.

Then, one day, as I was laying on my bunk, I begin to think about all I had accomplished while attending college and the work I had put into becoming a legitimate business man prior to this jolt. Instantly, I was struck with the reality of our situation, which then forced me to ask myself: If I left prison that day, what would I have to show for my efforts while incarcerated? Twenty cases of Top Ramen soups? Fuck!

Indeed, it was a moment of truth that, from that day forth, forced me to begin the long process of figuring out how I could, from a prison cell, get back on track to becoming a successful businessman. Of the many things I would have to do first, I had to readjust my focus by disciplining myself to reject much of the values that the streets and prison had put to me in terms of culture and limitations. Next, I would begin a study of my childhood, adulthood and environment so as to better understand not only how I had allowed it to shape my values but more so my limitations. Lastly, and this would result from my studies, I had to comb through all those bright ideas and experiences I had or had tried so that I could benefit from the insight and experience they had afforded me. That's when I struck gold!

Realizing there had been a plan all along that I had been developing, I now began to see clearly how it was I almost lost it in the chaos of my bad decisions. It was a plan born just weeks prior to me incidentally killing William.

I had just returned from visiting with my family in Oklahoma. While there, I had had a conversation with my uncle regarding how it was we had so much talent and resource in our family and community. Yet, in my opinion, it was not organized. That conversation would begin a long process that would eventually lead to me founding the United Black Family Scholarship Foundation (UBF).

The idea of starting a organization, a 501c3 nonprofit organization, from behind prison walls was not met with much fanfare. When I initially begin to look into what it would take to get it off the ground, my cellie, Shorty, flat-out said, "You cannot do it!" When I approached friends and family, many were encouraging and supporting of the idea. Yet they were not willing to assist with the work that it was involved in making an idea into a reality. Before long, I would realize I was not in an environment of possibilities and that I had quite a bit to learn in terms of surrounding myself with the right people and inspiring them to take action.

Of the first of many observations I was to make, was the ability of my story to inspire people. This, I would learn in time, provided me with a certain type of currency—a resource—that far exceeded the value of money in and of itself. Yeah life had dealt me a shitty hand. I was in prison sentenced to spend the rest of my days on earth locked in a cell. Still and yet, I possessed the ability to make a conscious decision to not allow these circumstances to define me or deter me from accomplishing my goals. Indeed, this was my gold!

In telling my story I was to learn in time that I was providing hope where there was none for many people. Seeing my ability to change and acknowledging the fact that change started with making a different choice, was powerful! With this I soon learned that in all my thinking, thinking I was without resource or the ability to influence people outside prison walls was a product of my ignorance that had hindered me from taking what the world had put before me and, as the adage goes, making lemonade.

This is when I realized that, in establishing the UBF, I would be creating not only my own opportunities, but so too those for others. So there I was lying on my bunk staring at the ceiling envisioning what this would look like. I had read somewhere that I would have to define what success would look like for me. Realizing I had but one value that had made all the difference in my ability to change, my experiences had taught me that that value was in the power of education. Success then would be defined in this organization's ability to educate people. Education not in the strict sense of credentialism, but rather education as it pertained to empowering people to deal critically and creatively with reality and discover how to participate in the transformation of their world.

That I was able to make this discovery and then create such an opportunity for myself and others has indeed been a humbling experience. For me personally, it has allowed for an experience to gain invaluable insight on everything from obtaining corporate funding to working with universities to establishing an internship program—all from a prison cell.

Where prison had once limited me in so many ways, I now had discovered a significant, no magnificent, ability to break the mental chains and debunk the myth that opportunities only come once in a lifetime. No! The truth is, we have to create our own opportunities by turning the key to release ourselves and our minds from the prisons that we construct between our own two ears.

---

[i] Kerness, B. "The Hidden History of Solitary Confinement In New Jersey Control Units." Solitary Watch, March 13, 2013.

[ii] Jamal, Sitawa N. et al. "Statement of California Prisoner Representatives on Second Anniversary of Ashker V. Brown Settlement." The Abolitionist, Winter 2018. Issue 28. Organizing Against Fascism, p.2.

[iii] Lussenhop, J. "Inmate Strikes Enter the Fray for U.S. Prison Reform." BBC News Magazine, October 3, 2016.

[iv] Wikipedia.org. Industrial Workers of the World, endnotes 77-80; see also SPR (2016) Strike Tracking & Retaliation Support. SupportPrisonResistance.net.

[v] Reutter, D.M. "Alabama Forced to Confront Criminal Justice Reform." Prison Legal News, May 2016; Vol. 27 No. 5.

[vi] Democracy Now! (2016). Alabama Guards Stage Work Strike Months After Prison Uprising at Overcrowded Holman Facility. DemocracyNow.org.

[vii] Ferris, K. & Jill Stein. The Real World: An Introduction to Sociology. W.W. Norton, 4th ed., pp. 477-78.